Published by Christian Focus Publications Ltd
Geanies House, Fearn, Tain, Ross-shire IV20 1TW www.christianfocus.com

Copyright © John Brown Brian Wright
ISBN: 978-1-5271-1166-0

This edition published in 2024
Cover illustration and internal illustrations by Lisa Flanagan
Cover and internal design by Lisa Flanagan
Printed and bound by Imprint, India

All rights reserved. No part of this publication may be reproduced, stored in a retrieval system, or transmitted, in any form, by any means, electronic, mechanical, photocopying, recording or otherwise without the prior permission of the publisher or a licence permitting restricted copying. In the U.K. such licences are issued by the Copyright Licensing Agency, 4 Battlebridge Lane, London, SE1 2HX. www.cla.co.uk

Amos &
God's roaring voice

John Brown
Brian Wright

In a land filled with rolling hills,
fruitful vineyards, and bustling cities,
there lived **a shepherd named Amos**.

Amos was a kind-hearted and humble man
who cared for his sheep with great love.
Most of his days were spent under the vast open sky,
protecting the sheep from danger.

But one day, while Amos was tending to his flock, the Lord God Almighty, Creator of heaven and earth, told Amos to **deliver some messages** to His people in the wealthy kingdom of Israel.

"The people have strayed far from the path of righteousness," God told Amos, "and their actions have caused pain and suffering. It is time for them to **hear the voice of justice.**"

Now the words Amos delivered to **the people of Israel** came two years before the big earthquake—the earthquake that shook Israel during the days of Uzziah, King of Judah.

As Amos walked down the busy streets throughout the land sharing God's message, he couldn't help but notice **the stark contrast** between the magnificent palaces of the rich and the rundown shelters of the poor.

And although the cities were alive with laughter, music, and feasting, Amos knew there was a **growing unhappiness and injustice** beneath the surface.

"**All of you** in the land
—from the Northeast to the Southwest,
and from the Northwest to the Southeast—
will be punished," Amos announced.

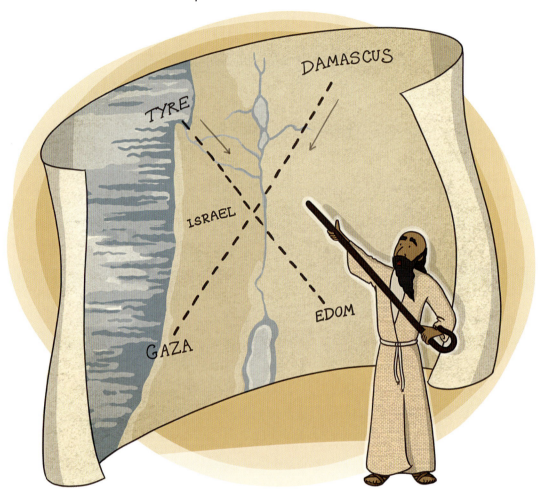

It was like God was drawing **a big X**
over the people's sin.

"God is going to burn down
everything you have built because
you have mistreated people,
rejected God's Word, and worshiped Him
without being sorry for what you have done."

Even though **God had been so kind** to His people—bringing them out of the land of Egypt, leading them for forty years in the wilderness, raising up some of their children to be God's special messengers—the northern tribes made their brothers and sisters in the south sin, they told God's prophets to be quiet, and they refused to hear the truth about how much they were displeasing God.

Amos then reminded Israel that
God had chosen them alone
—not any other nation—to be His people. And with this great privilege of being chosen as God's elect people, came the greater responsibility of living rightly before God.

"**God is surely coming** to judge you!"
Amos warned.

"He's not joking!"

But **the people would not listen** to Amos.

Not the women.

Not the men.

Not anyone.

But **God kept trying to get their attention**
—warning them through
difficult trials and sad times—
because He knew what was best for
their life: a trusting and obedient
relationship with Him.

"I held back the **rain**
so you would have no **grain**,"

"Yet you have not returned to Me."

"The clouds did not **burst**
so that you would **thirst**."

"Yet you have not returned to Me."

"I sent hot wind and moist **mold**,
and hungry bugs **untold**."

"Yet you have not returned to Me."

"I sent sickness and **sword**,
and foes by the **horde**."

"Yet you have not returned to Me."

"Therefore,
prepare to meet your God,
O Israel!"

At this point, Amos sang **a sad song** over Israel.

"O people of Israel, hear my **song**,
Truth and justice are fair and **strong**.
Our faithful Father looks down from **above**,
With tender eyes filled with **love**."

"Your houses may be grand and **tall**,
But do you hear the poor when they **call**?
They work hard and struggle day and **night**,
While you sit around enjoying your riches so **bright**."

"The Lord desires fairness and **grace**,
To see a smile on everyone's **face**.
Care for the needy, lend a **hand**,
For God Almighty will make justice **stand**."

"Beneath the stars, beneath the **skies**,
We seek His path where virtue **lies**,
'Seek the Lord and live,' our **creed**,
For in His justice, we find what we **need**."

"So let us strive, with hearts **aflame**,
To follow God's call and always honor His **name**,
'Seek the Lord and live,' our **guide**,
In pursuit of His justice, side by **side**."

But the people remained **complacent**, which means they were **lazy**.

And they stayed **self-absorbed**,
which means they
only cared about themselves.

So God planned on sending **locusts** to destroy their crops.

Then God announced that He would send **fire** to destroy their land.

But Amos cried out to God again,
"**Please have mercy** on them,
and don't send the fire!"

So **God answered his prayer**
and withheld the fire.

Then Amos saw the Lord holding **a measuring line** in His hand to see how His people measured up to His good and holy standards.

Whatever didn't measure up would be cut out.

Anything in their life that did not line up with His plumb line would be removed and destroyed.

"Indeed,
I will never pass over them again
like I did in Egypt."

Then Amos found himself standing in front of **God's temple**, where the people came to offer sacrifices and seek blessings. The temple was beautiful on the outside, but Amos knew the truth that was hidden on the inside.

"Hear the words of the Lord, O people of Israel! Your lavish feasts and grand offerings are empty gestures if your hearts are empty of compassion and fairness. You trample upon the poor and take advantage of the weak. **God desires justice** to flow down like a river and righteousness like a never-ending stream!"

"If you don't love your neighbors as yourselves," Amos warned, "you're not loving God. If you **love God**, then you will **love others** justly and righteously."

The people listened in astonishment as **Amos' words** pierced through their trickeries. Some laughed and mocked, but others felt a sense of guilt deep within their souls.

As Amos continued to speak, his voice grew stronger with each passing moment, especially since he knew God was going to send **Israel into exile**— away from their homes, friends, and communities.

"So prepare to say your **good-byes**,
for God sees through your **disguise**."

"But **there is still hope** for you,
O Israel! If you turn back to Him,
He will embrace you with His love.
He will restore your fortunes,
raise up the house of David,
and possess all the nations
who are called by His name."

Israel couldn't fully understand
the greatness of what God was pointing to
at this time, but we do now...

He was pointing to **Jesus Christ**—
the eternal Son of David, who is God's
promised King and true temple.

And one day, people from every nation,
from all tribes and peoples and languages,
will stand before Jesus saying,

"Salvation belongs to our God who sits on the throne, and to Jesus Christ!"

And so, the story of Amos and
God's roaring voice of justice
became the timeless Word of God that we still
read and obey to this day. And whoever believes
in Jesus Christ, will not be destroyed, but will
have everlasting life and all the blessings
that come with it.

"Never again will you be uprooted,"
says the Lord your God.

Christian Focus Publications publishes books for adults and children under its four main imprints: Christian Focus, CF4K, Mentor, and Christian Heritage. Our books reflect our conviction that God's Word is reliable and that Jesus is the way to know Him, and live for ever with Him.

Our children's publication list covers pre-school to early teens. We also publish personal and family devotionals, biographies and inspirational stories that children will love.

From pre-school board books to teenage apologetics, we have it covered!

Christian Focus Publications Ltd,
Geanies House, Fearn, Ross-shire,
IV20 1TW, Scotland,
United Kingdom.
www.christianfocus.com